PENGU

OF NEW ZEALAND

NH
NEW
HOLLAND

TEXT LLOYD SPENCER DAVIS
PHOTOGRAPHY ROD MORRIS

To the little red ship, and the lessons she taught us – RM
To John Darby, and the lessons he tried to teach us – LSD

First published in 2009 by New Holland Publishers (NZ) Ltd
Auckland • Sydney • London • Cape Town

www.newhollandpublishers.co.nz

218 Lake Road, Northcote, Auckland 0627, New Zealand
Unit 1, 66 Gibbes Street, Chatswood, NSW 2067, Australia
86–88 Edgware Road, London W2 2EA, United Kingdom
80 McKenzie Street, Cape Town 8001, South Africa

Publishing manager: Matt Turner
Edited by Bradstock & Associates, Christchurch
Designed by Cheryl Rowe
Maps: 5t NIWA, 5b Nick Keenleyside

Front cover photograph: Yellow-eyed penguin (hoiho)
Back cover photographs, from top: Fiordland penguin; king penguin; little penguins.

National Library of New Zealand Cataloguing-in-Publication Data

Davis, Lloyd Spencer, 1954-
Penguins of New Zealand / text, Lloyd Spencer Davis ;
photography, Rod Morris.
Family guide to New Zealand wildlife.
Includes bibliographical references and index.
ISBN 978-1-86966-261-5
1. Penguins—New Zealand. 2. Penguins—New Zealand—
Pictorial works. I. Morris, Rod, 1951- II. Title.
598.470993022—dc 22

10 9 8 7 6 5 4 3 2 1

Colour reproduction by Pica Digital Pte Ltd, Singapore
Printed by Times Offset (M) Sdn Bhd, Malaysia, on paper sourced from sustainable forests.

Photography/artwork: All images copyright Rod Morris with the exception of the following pages: 7
courtesy Dr R. Ewan Fordyce, Department of Geology, University of Otago; 8 Chris Gaskin, copyright
Geology Museum, University of Otago used with permission; 22 Lloyd Spencer Davis; 24, 26, 27, 56,
57 Kim Westerskov.

CONTENTS

Previous page: Little penguins. Above: King penguins take to the water in the flipper beats of their ancestors.

INTRODUCTION

A royal penguin, a white-faced subspecies of macaroni penguins, which breeds on Macquarie Island.

New Zealand is Penguin Central: the world capital of these fascinating birds. Of the 16 species of penguins living in the world today, nine can be found breeding in New Zealand or its territories (if we include the Ross Sea sector of Antarctica). And, if we wanted to get really picky, we'd add another three (the king, the gentoo, and the royal subspecies of macaroni penguin) that breed on Macquarie Island. For anyone looking at a topographical map of the Southern Ocean can clearly see that Macquarie Island is on an underwater ridge that extends from our Southern Alps like a sort of geographical umbilical cord. Also, the penguins of Macquarie – along with Magellanic penguins from South America – are frequent visitors to New Zealand. All this means that on any one day it is theoretically possible to have more than 80 per cent of the world's species of penguins represented in New Zealand.

Not only is New Zealand home to the greatest diversity of penguins alive today, the same was also true in the past. More fossil species have been described from the region than from any other, with no fewer than 20 species from mainland New Zealand alone. The first and the oldest fossil penguins hail from New Zealand also. It seems likely, then, that the New Zealand region is not just a home but *the* home of penguins – their birthplace and their place of origin, too.

A Snares penguin, one of four penguin species found only in New Zealand.

4

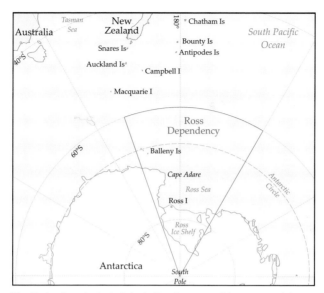

New Zealand's territories include the Ross Sea sector of Antarctica and the sub-Antarctic islands that lie in between.

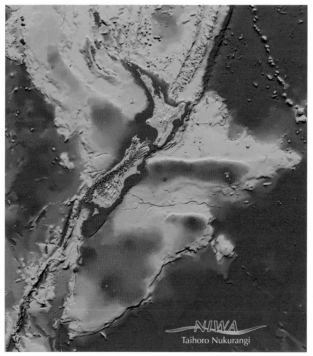

A hydrographic map showing the extent of the largely submarine continent of Zealandia.

NEW ZEALAND PENGUINS OF THE PAST

Kahikatea swamp. Prehistoric New Zealand at the time penguins evolved was covered in forest.

New Zealand and its geological history

If you look at a map of New Zealand what do you see? A couple of big islands (named, with all the romance for which Kiwi blokes are famous, as the North Island and South Island), one modest-sized one at the bottom (Stewart Island), and a group of tiny hangers-on widely scattered around their bigger brethren. The classic story was that New Zealand broke away from Australia some tens of millions of years ago, like a little Noah's Ark that carried only a few passengers. As New Zealand drifted eastwards, its rather limited cargo of itinerants then evolved to fill ecological niches that were vacant in the absence of a larger cast of characters. New Zealand was, according to the story the scientists told us, devoid of predatory mammals, dinosaurs, snakes and crocodiles, so birds had little need for flight and some gave it up altogether in exchange for a more down-to-earth lifestyle. Moa, kiwi, takahe and kakapo: a litany of famous names that head the list of New Zealand's characteristically aerially-challenged avifauna.

It's a great story, but has one significant imperfection: it's wrong.

New Zealand is but an emergent pimple of an enormous, largely submerged continent known as Zealandia. Once it was part of Gondwanaland, that collection of the world's landmasses that congregated in the south before drifting apart to form South America, Africa, India, Australia and Antarctica. Recently, scientists have realised that there was another bit to Gondwanaland – another continent – that broke off from Australia about 83 million years ago and then spent the following 60 million years slowly sinking until hardly any of it stuck above the surface. Zealandia was about ten times the size of modern New Zealand and can be seen clearly in underwater topographic maps, stretching from Campbell Island in the south to New Caledonia in the north.

The animals and plants that originally lived on the 'mother ship' Zealandia were a fair cross-section of those found on Gondwanaland. Virtually every major animal and plant group was represented. Recent fossil discoveries reveal that at one time New Zealand did indeed have dinosaurs and mammals, snakes and crocodiles. Something catastrophic must have happened to eventually reduce Zealandia's passengers to a rag-tag collection of refugees. It seems likely that by about 23 million years ago nearly all of Zealandia had sunk, leaving a few tenuous toeholds and a limited range of habitats. Geology and water had dealt a blow to New Zealand's biodiversity in a way that evolutionary competition could not. Perhaps more thanks to good luck than good genes, some species survived on the small number of left-over islands while other lineages simply died out as their habitats dwindled. When some of the land resurfaced, in the shapes we recognise as New Zealand today, the survivors were a much-reduced collection of Zealandia's original plants and animals. It was a new story but with a familiar ending: the New Zealand land birds would become flightless in the absence of competitors and predators.

Meanwhile, on the coasts of New Zealand, another group of birds had been dispensing with flight for completely different reasons.

New Zealand fossil penguins

Penguins evolved from flying birds – of that we can be certain – and it seems that their ancestors last flew a little more than 60 million years ago. We can say this with some confidence because a fossil bird was recently unearthed from a layer of deposits known as the Waipara Greensand.

Waipara is an area about 50 kilometres north of Christchurch that is renowned for its vineyards. Yet for palaeontologists the best thing to have come from the land is not a wine but an almost complete fossil skeleton. Painstakingly extracted from

Dr Ewan Fordyce, University of Otago, with fossils of Platydyptes, *an Oligocene penguin uncovered at Earthquakes, near Duntroon in the Waitaki valley.*

Reconstructions suggest that early penguins like Platydyptes *had quickly evolved to already look much like modern penguins. This scene depicts a coastal Otago of around 25 million years ago.*

the soils of Waipara and recently christened *Waimanu manneringi* by the scientists, the fossil is the latest addition to New Zealand's list of birds that cannot fly. Except that *Waimanu* was different from the kiwis and moas and the rest of the wingless wonders on that list: it was clearly a diver, not a walker; a swimmer, not a runner. It was, to all intents and purposes, a penguin.

Several different techniques of dating *Waimanu* all tell the same story: this primordial penguin lived a little over 60 million years ago. *Waimanu* has features consistent with both the aquatic lifestyle of modern-day penguins and attributes more commonly associated with flying. It may not be the missing link, but it is clearly close enough to the transition from flier to swimmer that it still carries with it some of the architecture of a former existence.

Given that Zealandia was formed some 83 million years ago, the finding of a 60-million-year-old fossil of a 'prototype' penguin suggests rather strongly that penguins evolved in the New Zealand region.

If the discovery of *Waimanu* would appear to cement New Zealand's place in the world as the hotbed of penguin evolution, it only confirms what had already been suggested by a fossil found nearly a century and a half earlier. In one of palaeontology's quirkiest stories, 300 kilometres south of Waipara, the son of Gideon Mantell, the man who found the world's first dinosaur fossil, was to unearth the world's first penguin fossil (see box opposite).

MANTELL'S MARVELLOUS METATARSUS

In 1848, Walter Mantell, acting as Commissioner for 'extinguishing native claims in the Middle Island', acquired a strange broken bit of bone unearthed from the limestone deposits around Kakanui on the North Otago coastline. He sent it back to Britain, where it ended up in the hands of Thomas Huxley, best known for being Charles Darwin's champion –'Darwin's Bulldog' they called him – but also a man who knew his way around old bones. In 1859, the same year Darwin published *On the Origin of Species*, Huxley published a scientific paper describing Mantell's fossil bone as the tarsometatarsal (fused ankle bone) of an extinct penguin, on which he bestowed the name *Palaeeudyptes antarcticus* (meaning 'ancient winged diver of the south').

But how could he tell it was a penguin from just one bone – and a broken bone at that? Quite fortuitously, the tarsometatarsus is the most distinctive bone that penguins possess, so Huxley could rule out dinosaurs, crocodiles, mammals, snakes and whatever else might have been around at the time. Also, the bone was much more dense and solid than the hollow bones of flying birds, so the bird it came from must have been flightless. Bones without air spaces are characteristic of penguins and help them to dive by counteracting the buoyancy

of water. So it was not as if Huxley had to be an Einstein to figure things out. Unfortunately, though, no other verified specimens of *Palaeeudyptes antarcticus* have ever been found, so that all that is known of the world's first-discovered fossil penguin species is that which can be gleaned from a single damaged ankle bone lying in a drawer in the Natural History Museum in London.

It seemed that, for a long while, every man and his dog that happened upon a fossil penguin bone, whether in New Zealand, Australia or Antarctica, was tempted to call it *Palaeeudyptes*, if not *antarcticus* also. However, re-examination of the bones shows that many belong in a whole new group of large penguins living some 27–29 million years ago around what is today the Waihao River in South Canterbury and the Duntroon area in North Otago. This group is known collectively as 'the Waihao penguin' and whatever multi-syllabic mouthful may be eventually bestowed upon it, that name will then be passed on to all the pretenders to the *P. antarcticus* throne.

From the age of the limestone deposits around Kakanui, it is likely that the actual *P. antarcticus* lived somewhere between 23 and 34 million years ago: old, though not by *Waimanu* standards, and certainly not as old as birds come.

Candidates for the nearest living relatives of penguins: frigatebirds (top) and albatross.

Penguin predecessors

What were the ancestors of penguins? The evidence is contradictory. Penguins could have arisen from ancestors that were like petrels, storks, frigate birds, or loons. All we know for sure is that their ancestors could fly. Many think the albatross and petrels are the closest living relatives, if for no other reason than they share similar distribution, diet, and breeding behaviour. They sort of look like what you might *imagine* a flying penguin would if you could magically wave a wand and give it wings.

At first glance loons would appear to be unlikely candidates because, unlike penguins, they are propelled by their feet, not their wings, when they dive – but there is evidence that loons are themselves descended from wing-propelled diving ancestors. Indeed, reconstructions of *Waimanu* and the early penguins do show a superficial resemblance to loons.

Relationships of modern penguins

The 16 species of penguin alive today represent only a fraction of the different species of penguins that have lived on Earth, and, in fact, it seems that none of the species alive today go back more than three million years. So in evolutionary terms they are young: older than *Homo sapiens* for sure, but younger than some of the other crusty old creatures like tuatara, which survived Zealandia's near-burial at sea. The living species of penguins fall into six genera (the plural of genus): *Spheniscus*, *Eudyptula*, *Megadyptes*, *Eudyptes*, *Aptenodytes* and *Pygoscelis*. Only *Spheniscus* does not have any members breeding in New Zealand, although Magellanic penguins (*Spheniscus mendiculus*) from South America occasionally waddle up a New Zealand beach looking for some R&R.

Most *Spheniscus* penguins (the Humboldt, African and Galápagos penguins) are creatures of warmer climates, breeding in the subtropical and tropical zones. The fourth, the Magellanic penguin, lives further south. All penguins live in the southern hemisphere, but the Galápagos penguin breeds on the Galápagos Islands, right on the equator. So they may even venture a few metres into the northern hemisphere, but no one's going to let that get in the way of a good generalisation: penguins are exclusively southern hemisphere birds. (This is also why they never co-exist with polar bears – except in the imagination of cartoonists.)

Two of the genera, *Eudyptula* and *Megadyptes*, have only a single living representative: the little and yellow-eyed penguins respectively. There has been some argument about whether the white-flippered penguin, a variant of the little penguin that breeds largely around Banks Peninsula and on Motunau Island north of Christchurch, is a separate species. However, the evidence – morphologic, behavioural, genetic – all points to it being just a local variety or subspecies of little penguin. White-flippered penguins interbreed freely with other little penguins.

The Fiordland, Snares, erect-crested and rockhopper penguins all belong to the genus *Eudyptes* – the crested penguins, with yellowish plumes of feathers above their eyes, like eyebrows on steroids. There is only one other living *Eudyptes* species, the macaroni penguin, but this is absent from New Zealand, although a subspecies of macaroni penguin, known as the royal penguin, breeds on Macquarie Island and geographically is probably part of the New Zealand fauna anyway, even if the Australians own it.

Emperor penguins breed in the Ross Sea sector of Antarctica and along other parts of the Antarctic coastline. They share the generic name *Aptenodytes* with king penguins, which occupy a band around the sub-Antarctic, although the closest they get to breeding in New Zealand is on Macquarie too.

If New Zealand could claim the gentoo penguins that breed on Macquarie, we could also declare a full house for the three members of the genus *Pygoscelis*. The Adélie penguin is very numerous at colonies scattered along the coast and islands of the Ross Sea. Although the chinstrap penguin is found mostly around the Antarctic Peninsula, on the other side of Antarctica to New Zealand, a small colony of chinstrap penguins insists on breeding on the Balleny Islands – the most isolated and god-forsaken excuse for a breeding site one could hope to find between New Zealand and the South Pole. Even today, the number of people who have landed on the Balleny Islands could probably be counted on the remaining fingers of one frost-bitten hand.

Even though genetics and morphology can't resolve which groups of other birds are most closely related to penguins, they help with determining how the penguins relate to each other: *Spheniscus* penguins are closely related to *Eudyptula*, *Megadyptes* close to *Eudyptes*, and *Pygoscelis* close to *Aptenodytes*. There is 100 per cent agreement on that. Things start to get a little murkier when trying to decide which is the oldest living species or how they may be descended from each other. DNA analysis suggests

A white-flippered penguin, a subspecies of the little penguin, reveals the white margins that give rise to its name.

Adélie penguins live and breed exclusively in Antarctica.

either *Aptenodytes* or *Pygoscelis* as the oldest, and it also just happens that both breed only in the Antarctic or sub-Antarctic. This is clearly a derived condition, given that penguins arose at a time and place when conditions were temperate to subtropical. By way of contrast, morphological evidence points to *Spheniscus* being most ancient. In a sense none of this really matters because, when the fossil penguins are factored in too, it seems clear that even though *Spheniscus* may be closer to ancestral penguins like *Waimanu*, too many of the branches that connect the modern penguins to the first penguins are missing. We are unable to reconstruct anything other than a sketched outline of the penguins' evolutionary tree, and certainly not the individual branching pathways that evolution took.

Flyer to diver: an evolutionary compromise

Birds first evolved as a branch of the dinosaurs about 150 million years ago. And you have to ask yourself, if they were happy enough flying about for nearly 90 million years, what made some of them want to pack away the wings and put on the avian equivalent of a mask, snorkel and flippers? Flying would seem to be better for several reasons, not least being an ability to get you from A to B to get food in double-quick time without climbing uphill and over other terrestrial obstacles, and to keep you out of the reach of predators lurking on the ground.

All that supposes you live off the land … but what if you like seafood?

Now turn your attention to all those birds flitting about in the Cretaceous skies, around the time the dinosaurs and many other lifeforms met their demise, but before any of the mammals had begun to evolve into creatures that could move back into the ocean. The seas must have represented a giant dinner plate to any birds that could feed in the water. Cue the albatross, petrels, frigate birds, the auk and the like.

Trouble is, the requirements for diving to find food are exactly opposite to those of flight. Flying requires a light body with a big surface area for the wings to provide lift; and the heavier the bird, the greater the surface area needs to be. But diving works best when the animal is heavy and has short, powerful wings that can act like paddles to counteract the buoyancy of water. Not only that, but birds breathe with lungs not gills, so that the deeper they need to go, the more oxygen they need to store, which in turn means they need to be bigger. To access food at depth, simple physics dictates that the best designs will need to be big and heavy with short, stiff wings. Fortunately birds don't need to do the maths: evolution has done it for them, with the critical value being about 1 kilogram. Any heavier and they can't be both a flyer and diver.

This is why diving seabirds like auks that tip the scales at 600–900 grams can still fly, if modestly. However, anything bigger has to give up flight in exchange for whatever advantages diving may bring it. (The extinct Great Auk weighed around 5 kilograms … and, unsurprisingly, was flightless.) Conversely, it also explains why the smallest extinct penguins ever found and the smallest penguins alive today weigh about 1 kg: that's the weight at which the move from wings to flippers makes evolutionary sense.

Once they had given up being both divers and flyers, the earliest penguins could then grow to any size. Sixty million years ago *Waimanu* was already big – waist-high – and probably could dive to great depths. Another fossil penguin stood over 1.7 metres tall: it didn't so much dive as free-fall. And, since at that stage they didn't have to share their watery world with marine mammals, they were able to evolve rapidly into many distinct species.

This transition from flyer to diver was as significant as that from knuckle-walker to upright bipedal walker for humans. Just as freeing our hands opened up many possibilities for our ancestors, becoming divers and embracing an aquatic existence did the same for penguins. But it would be wrong to think of the change as being entirely positive. The penguins had to forgo the advantages of flight and, encumbered with a body designed for water, they faced difficulties when on land.

Penguins could not return to the ocean completely and become like fish. A female mammal can nurture her developing embryos and swim at the same time, but birds lay eggs. They evolved to get their embryos out of the body at an early stage in development so the additional payload didn't weigh them down when they flew. The eggs of birds are porous, to allow oxygen to get in and carbon dioxide to get out, so they are not waterproof. And the eggs must be kept warm. If only because penguins laid permeable eggs that needed incubating, they were always destined to be tied to the land for breeding.

And there was another reason anyway. Penguins have to come ashore every year to moult – to shed their old, worn feathers and replace them with brand new ones.

Unable to leave their old world behind and enter their new world fully, penguins have been forced to live a compromised existence in two worlds.

A king penguin: too heavy to fly but perfect for diving deep.

LIFE ON LAND

King penguins negotiate elephant seals as they come ashore.

The image of penguins we are all familiar with is colonies of them ashore, but this is a misrepresentation to some extent – like trying to understand our lives by observing us only in our bedrooms. Penguins spend the vast majority of their lives at sea. Ashore they are somewhat like fish out of water.

Somehow, they need to select a breeding site, find a mate, rear their offspring and renew their feather suits on land, yet all the while these activities must be fuelled by energy that they get from the sea.

Selecting a breeding site

Rule #1: The closer to the sea, the better

On land, penguins are reduced to walking – or, where snow and ice permits, sliding on their bellies. Their stubby legs, upright stance and waddling gait mean that they seem to walk funny. They take tiny steps for such big birds. Think of penguins onshore as taking part in a perpetual sack race and you will get some insight into just how inefficient their means of locomotion is on land. This reduces how far they can reasonably travel.

So: the first rule for penguin breeding sites is that they must be close to shore. Within waddling distance. This restricts most to less than a kilometre or two from the coast, and usually they are much closer than that even.

Evolution has co-opted the penguins' feathers to perform the necessary insulation that was really the key to their becoming the most aquatic of all seabirds – the ones most deserving of the title 'seabirds'.

The layer of feathers over the body of penguins is three times thicker than on flying birds. The feathers are distributed evenly across the skin rather than in tracts, as is the norm for flying birds. They are symmetrical (whereas the feathers of flying birds are asymmetrical), stiff, stubby, and lock together with little hooks like millions of pieces of Velcro, thereby trapping an insulating layer of air against the skin of the penguin.

Rule #2: Shelter from the sun, not the storm

Penguins have a core body temperature of about 39°C, actually a couple of degrees hotter than ourselves. The problem for them is to stay warm in water (which conducts heat away from the body 25 times faster than air) but not to get too hot on land. Other warm-blooded creatures have evolved suitable insulation for a marine life by having masses of fat (e.g. whales), fur (e.g. polar bears), or both (e.g. seals), but birds have evolved to be lean and light for flying. (They do have significant fat stores in specific parts of their bodies, but these are used mainly as energy reserves to sustain long periods of fasting when on shore.)

It's a penguin's survival suit of feathers that keeps it snug in the coldest water, but this has a downside when on shore as it can overheat. Keeping warm on land is usually not a problem but keeping *too* warm is. Penguins breeding on mainland New Zealand solve this in several ways. Yellow-eyed penguins breed in coastal forest where they can keep out of the sun. Little penguins come ashore after it gets dark, and most nest in burrows or caves. Fiordland penguins breed in rainforests, under other vegetation and in any caves they can find. (They also breed in winter, when it's cooler.)

Further south, as it gets colder, the problem of overheating lessens. This is why penguins breeding on the sub-Antarctic islands and in the Antarctic itself can nest in the open, forming colonies with nests cheek by jowl as other colonial seabirds do.

Snares penguins form small colonies spread throughout the *Olearia* forests of the Snares Islands, where they nest surrounded by trees rather than seeking shelter beneath them. Snares penguins often roost in the branches of the trees – unfamiliar territory for penguins since before the time of *Waimanu*. Erect-crested penguins cling to rocky platforms, typically devoid of any vegetation, on the Bounty and Antipodes Islands. So do rockhopper penguins on our sub-Antarctic islands. While many of New Zealand's penguins breed exclusively in New Zealand, rockhoppers are cosmopolitan characters and can be found breeding in many places that ring the sub-Antarctic.

In Antarctic waters, we find an errant colony of chinstrap penguins that breed in the open on the Balleny Islands. Adélie penguins breed on the Antarctic continent proper, and on its offshore islands, where they need areas of land that are free of snow. Here they make their nests as scrapes in the ground that they line with small stones to elevate the eggs and protect

Chinstrap penguins, which breed in Antarctica, have less reason than some to protect themselves from overheating.

them from meltwater. In one sense they are the most extreme penguins because their colony at Cape Royds (77°38'S) is the furthest south that any bird breeds. But when it comes to doing it hard, it seems that the Adélies always get trumped by the emperors.

Emperors are too big (up to 38 kilograms) to rear a chick in the Antarctic summer because, while food may be plentiful then, time is short. As a consequence, and crazy though it may sound, the only way they can do it is to start the breeding process early, so they start breeding in winter. There are no snow-free nest sites on land at that time of year, so emperor penguins breed on the frozen sea ice and do not use nest sites as such. Instead they carry their single egg on their feet, covered by a flap from their bellies which they wrap round the egg like a built-in electric blanket. They also huddle together, sharing their body warmth and forming a partial barrier to the winds.

Penguins didn't start out as creatures of the ice and snow: they evolved in the subtropical to temperate climates of Zealandia back in *Waimanu*'s day. When they first made it to Antarctica, it was warmer than it is now, and covered with forests. But things cooled fairly rapidly after the circumpolar Antarctic Current started up about 30 million years ago. Most birds moved out of the neighbourhood or died out, but penguins stayed as they were pre-equipped with their feather survival suits to cope with the change.

Rule #3: Inshore or offshore

Penguins don't eat when ashore, so the part of the sea where they get their food must be close enough for them to reach it while still managing to mate and raise their eggs and chicks.

Just *how* far a penguin must travel to reach its food affects almost every aspect of its life. In fact penguins can be roughly divided into two categories with very

Humboldt penguins in Peru typically manage to find enough food close to shore.

King penguins must sometimes find a mate that, if not one in a million, is one in several hundred thousand.

different life history traits based upon how far they forage: *inshore* feeders and *offshore* feeders.

Inshore feeders generally forage within 20 kilometres of their nest and tend to live at the colony year-round. Males and females take turns on the nest, changing over every 1–2 days. Overall, they start breeding younger (3 years on average) than offshore feeders (6 years on average), and tend to remain more faithful to their partners, because they stick together a lot on the land, reinforcing the pair bond.

Offshore feeders often travel 100 kilometres or more during the incubation period and stay away for two or more weeks at a time. When the chicks hatch, the parents must forage closer inshore to keep them well fed, but they still tend to take longer at sea and go further from the colony than inshore feeders.

Looking at the New Zealand penguins, the yellow-eyed penguin is an inshore feeder, the little penguin swings both ways (inshore or offshore depending upon its location), and all the rest are offshore feeders.

Finding a mate

Being forced to turn up at a colony for breeding has its advantages when it comes to getting a mate: it's not as though you need to wonder where to start looking. And since penguins know when it's time to breed by the changing daylength, prospective partners tend to show up about the same time as you. (Of course, so will your competitors, and therein lies the rub.)

WHY PENGUINS LOOK THE SAME

Penguins, like most self-respecting colonial seabirds, are *monomorphic*, which means males and females both look the same or nearly so. Penguins can't always tell a male from a female by simply glancing at it. This can lead to some gross errors – and, indeed, male Adélie penguins breeding on Ross Island have been known to mount the occasional unsuspecting male lying on the ground catching forty winks. Males don't show much discrimination when breeding (this is almost universal in the animal kingdom and is a consequence of males being able to produce sperm by the millions so wastage is of little concern), while females are much more selective because they produce only a few eggs, so they make sure they don't squander their precious few breeding opportunities. This is why among most animals the males go to all sorts of lengths to fight for and attract the attention of available females: from elaborate songs to adornments like large tail feathers or big horns, to bright and beautiful coloration. The more successful these devices are in producing mating opportunities, the stronger is the pressure of natural selection to have such traits. As a consequence, over time males tend to become different in appearance from the females of those species, which are said to be sexually dimorphic. But it's not so straightforward in cases where hard work and commitment by *both* parents is necessary to successfully rear the young. That situation encourages having just one mate (monogamy) and, with about 50/50 males/females in the population, it means nearly all males get to breed so there is no strong advantage for them to be more showy compared with other males. Consequently, for birds like penguins, monomorphism goes hand in hand with monogamy.

For a long time people thought that female seabirds, like penguins, pretty much took whatever was on offer and then stayed bonded to that partner for the rest of their natural lives. It was like an idealised version of human marriage.

But if ever a scientific concept was bound to be proved even more wrong than the pre-Zealandia views of New Zealand, it was that males of any species, let alone penguins, had a natural tendency to be faithful to their mates. In fact the surprise, if there is one, is discovering female penguins are not averse to a little infidelity.

So let's clear up the misconceptions once and for all: penguins do *not* mate for life! For some, like the emperor penguins, it's pretty much all they can do to stay with the same partner for one season. Forget *March of the Penguins*: emperor penguins have a 'divorce' rate of over 90 per cent from one year to the next.

The most detailed studies on the mating behaviour of penguins have been carried out on Adélie penguins in the New Zealand sector of Antarctica. The first thing scientists discovered was that 30–50 per cent of penguins changed partners from one season to the next, and, surprisingly, while they take only one partner at a time, about a third of them change partners during the season. Some males and females can even have three or more partners in a single season, like the bird equivalent of *Desperate Housewives*.

Perhaps because watching penguins mate was too unseemly, or the act too fleeting, or they were just clinging to a romantic myth, for a long time scientists had missed what was really going on. Eventually a group of arguably masochistic and voyeuristic New Zealand scientists on Ross Island watched penguins mating around the clock in the 24-hour daylight of the Antarctic summer, and discovered that quite a few female penguins would have a bit of sex on the side when their own partner was not looking. This wasn't swapping mates as

Mating for male penguins, such as these gentoo penguins, requires a fair degree of balance.

such, and it could potentially result in the females duping their partners into helping to rear offspring of which they might not be the father.

Yet there was more. Some female Adélies were observed having sex with unpaired males apparently in exchange for a stone, which they then took back to their own partner to help build their nest – introducing the unlikely term 'working girl' to penguin biology.

Suffice to say that the supposed monogamy of penguins is overstated. In fact, when it comes to sex they are a lot more like us than we supposed them to be.

Other penguins have not been studied as closely, but mate-swapping has also been observed in New Zealand's Fiordland and erect-crested penguins. In the Humboldt penguins of South America, about 30 per cent of the females have 'extra-pair copulations' (what we would call quickies on the side).

Traditionally, in other seabirds, there is some advantage to staying with a partner: practice and experience typically count for a lot in the bird world. It seems that the inclination among penguins to answer the door whenever opportunity knocks is inversely related to how hostile and how seasonal is the environment in which they breed. Those breeding furthest south, like Adélies, have a very short season during which conditions are right for breeding, so they cannot afford to wait around for a partner – even a proven partner – if it means they could miss out altogether on the opportunity to breed.

At the other extreme, yellow-eyed penguins live together at their colony pretty much all year round. This reinforces the pair bond and means they are seldom too far from each other. The result: while not mating for life, yellow-eyed penguins are certainly a lot more faithful to their partners than other New Zealand penguins.

Penguin calls

Male penguins attract females by calling, whether it is their first time breeding or they are just on the lookout for more mating opportunities. The call of males is sometimes referred to as the 'ecstatic call' and the whole package of call and display is known as the 'ecstatic display'. (This is a rather inappropriate term for several

Even the Galápagos penguin can make calls that are louder and harsher than its diminutive size would suggest.

reasons: it suggests that penguins feel emotion; and, even if they did, they usually call when unpaired; also, to our ears they sound more like they are in pain than the throes of ecstasy.) Penguin calls are hardly melodic. Most penguins make harsh cries that fall somewhere between a honk and a scream – often repeated over and over. Only yellow-eyed penguins seem to have a certain musicality and rhythm, while the call of an emperor penguin is more haunting than harsh.

Male little penguins will call at the entrances to their nest burrows, or collectively in a cave if they happen to be nesting in one. However, some little penguins find that the area underneath a house makes a pretty good substitute for a cave – especially around Eastbourne on the north-eastern side of Wellington Harbour. If it sounds appealing to have penguins nesting under your house, it is something you soon get tired of, especially if they are in a romantic mood. Their incessant calling has been known to drive some people out of their houses.

Females tend to prefer males with deeper voices, probably because these are also the larger males, which are more likely to have bigger fat stores, giving them more to come and go on when looking after the eggs and chicks. One of the primary constraints of trying to feed in one world and breed in another is that when penguins are at the nest they are on an enforced fast. An important part of being a successful breeder is withstanding the periods of fasting when ashore to incubate eggs or brood chicks.

Incubation

Being big helps with being a diver (see p. 12). But it also takes longer to develop

and grow up into a large bird than, say, some scrawny sparrow. This means that penguin eggs must be incubated for a long time (always more than a month) followed by a long period of being fed and protected before the chick can become an independent adult. It's all too much for one parent to do alone so bi-parental care is a necessity.

The parents must co-ordinate between themselves when each is going to be at the nest, alternating attendance so that when one is on the nest the other is at sea getting food. Spend too long at sea and your partner may get too hungry

Yellow-eyed penguins have the most variable incubation period of any penguin.

and desert the nest, or your chicks may starve; spend too little time and you may not accumulate the fat reserves necessary to endure fasting when it's your turn on the nest. It's a tricky balancing act called 'co-ordination of nest relief', and studies of little penguins in New Zealand and Adélie penguins in the Ross Sea have demonstrated that this balance is one of the most important factors influencing breeding success. The only more important thing is protecting the egg or chick from predators.

For penguins that feed close to their colony, like yellow-eyed penguins, co-ordination of nest relief is relatively easy, as each parent is typically away from the nest for only a day or two at a time. However, all the other New Zealand penguins go to sea for 1–2 weeks or even longer during incubation, and female emperors

leave their male partners for the entire 2 months the egg takes to hatch. Little penguins can take both short and long trips away, depending upon where they are breeding. At Oamaru, they seldom go off to sea for more than a day or two; in the Marlborough Sounds they can be away for more than a week.

The various species of crested penguins are different from all the rest. For reasons that are difficult to fathom, once their eggs are laid, both male and female stay together on the nest for 10 days or more. This seems bizarre because only one of

Successful breeding requires both parents to help out, as is the case with these macaroni penguins.

them can incubate at a time, so it would make sense for one of them to go and feed during this period. But no: they insist on hanging out together until the male eventually decides he's had enough and goes to sea, leaving the female on her own for another couple of weeks. (Except that, in the case of Fiordland penguins, it's the female who goes to sea first.) Why the male doesn't depart earlier and spare his partner from the extended fast is not clear. The best explanation so far is that he hangs around to protect his partner from other penguins. Because crested penguins are bullies. Unpaired erect-crested and Snares penguins go around like bovver boys, pecking incubating females and beating them with their flippers, sometimes causing them to abandon the nest and lose their eggs.

Clutch size

Penguins most often lay a clutch of two eggs, but king and emperor penguins lay just one. Usually the eggs are laid 3 or 4 days apart and are about the same size, though the first may be a smidgen bigger. Again, the crested penguins are the odd ones out: they take 4–6 days to lay the second egg and it can be much bigger than the first. If both eggs of a crested penguin hatch – and often they do not – it is typically the chick from the second-laid egg that hatches first, despite its late start in the world. And here's the kicker: even though all crested penguin species lay two eggs, they only ever rear one chick. Most often it is the chick from the second egg that survives. Why they should lay two eggs when they only ever rear one is a question that has baffled bird biologists for decades.

The first-laid eggs of erect-crested penguins (top) are substantially smaller than those laid second.

There has even been a suggestion that erect-crested penguins breeding on the Antipodes and Bounty Islands deliberately eject their first egg from the nest when the second one is laid. However, research has revealed that it is not so much a case of deliberate ejection as bad parenting and poor housekeeping. Nest-building is not the forte of erect-crested penguins: they lay the eggs on bare rock. They usually push the bigger egg into the brood patch first and then try to roll the small egg in too. The disparity of size between the eggs is such that the small egg is easily dislodged and rolls from the nest – or non-nest, as the case may be.

Causes of demise

Little penguins and Adélies often desert eggs because their partner is at sea too long. If one parent is away when the chicks hatch, the incubating parent is unlikely to have anything left in its stomach to regurgitate, and any chick that is not fed will

A giant petrel grabs a king penguin chick while an adult penguin and sheathbill look on.

starve to death within a few days. Timing is especially crucial for the survival of an emperor penguin chick, where the incubating male parent will not have eaten for about three and a half months by the time the egg hatches. If the mother does not show up with dinner, the father can actually produce a milk-like substance to feed his hungry charge. It's called oesophageal milk, and the male manufactures it by literally breaking down his own tissues, then regurgitating bits of himself to his chick.

The biggest threat eggs and chicks face is usually predators. In the Antarctic and sub-Antarctic that usually means other seabirds like skuas and fulmars. In New Zealand, it can mean introduced predators like cats, stoats, ferrets and weasels. Fiordland penguins are even vulnerable to having their eggs eaten by weka – another of New Zealand's flightless native birds. Dogs may also be a problem when penguins breed close to human habitation, with little penguins and yellow-eyed penguins most at risk.

Surprisingly, penguins are so well adapted to the harsh climates in which they breed that it is comparatively rare for eggs and chicks to die from the weather or cold. Burrow-nesters like little penguins may occasionally lose eggs or chicks to floods after heavy rain.

Once the chick or chicks have grown to a certain size, both parents start to go away simultaneously from the nest to get food for their ever-demanding young. During this stage, chicks of colonial penguins may congregate in groups called crèches. These help provide protection from predators and, especially in the Antarctic, close physical contact may help keep them warm in bad weather – emperor chicks most of all.

When at last the chicks are left to fend for themselves, they fledge by going into the water. Their apparent awkwardness and vulnerability disappears at once as their streamlined body shape and other adaptations for an aquatic life now come to the fore. This is where, for the first time, it becomes clear why their ancestors traded water for wings, and a slim figure for a rotund one.

LIFE IN WATER

Underwater, penguins look more fish-like than bird-like.

Water is a pretty unforgiving medium to move around in. It's a lot denser than air so it creates resistance, meaning it takes more energy to travel the same distance. As a consequence, there is a strong selective pressure for animals to evolve body designs that make moving through the water easier. And when it comes to moving through water, time and time again one design has proved superior. Look at the shape of most fish, and the shape of penguins: it's no coincidence that they're similar. The spindle-shape design which so characterises most of them is faster and more efficient. They get to eat more, to be eaten less, to breed more and to eventually leave more offspring than their competitors. The physics of moving through water dictates that this one particular design will triumph in the competition of natural selection. On land, penguins may have had a certain amount of latitude in body form and function, but when they went into the sea they swapped that freedom for conformity.

Therein lies the joke. Penguins *are* all conformists; they *do* all look alike to some extent. But it was the sea that made them that way. You could just as easily say the same about salmon, dolphins or seals. Yet, for some reason, cartoonists have made a big deal out of the apparent lack of individuality among penguins.

There's no point developing a streamlined body shape if you have bits hanging off it that are going to massively increase drag and undo all that good design work. If penguins were designed by some 20-year-old with an iMac sitting on a Swiss ball in some sparsely furnished designer's office in Wellington, you could imagine him turning to his boss and saying, 'No, the legs have got to go.' And, in a sense, evolution came to the same conclusion. That is, the design that proved the most efficient was to reduce the legs to the minimum and put them down the back end, where they'd be out of the way when swimming and could even function as a rudder.

So there we have it: the penguin that we love so much on land is really that way because natural selection designed it to live in water. Perhaps what is most amazing is that no human designer has ever been able to match what evolution has produced by way of the penguin. Tests in wind tunnels and flume tanks show that penguins have a lower coefficient of drag than *any* vehicle designed by humans.

Food

None of this biological re-engineering, from stork or albatross to super-submarine, would make any sense unless there were rewards for making that change – and it seems a fair bet that food was the primary driver of penguin design.

Penguins of all sizes are partial to small schooling fish, but will eat whatever they can get. The crucial thing is that they favour the type of food found in dense groups. For little penguins that may well be small schooling fish like pilchards and sardines. Others, like Fiordland penguins, may favour squid or krill. It depends on what is available.

The diets of many of our sub-Antarctic crested penguins are not especially well known, but probably consist of fish, krill and squid. One study of Snares penguins found they took juvenile pipefish when close to the colony. But who knows what they were feeding on when further afield?

Chinstrap and Adélie penguins around the Antarctic Peninsula usually feed almost entirely on krill, but in the Ross Sea a significant proportion of the Adélie penguin diet is Antarctic silverfish. Sometimes fish even dominate their diet. Emperors also feed on squid, as well as lanternfish, common mid-water fishes of the deep sea, which are also eaten by king penguins.

King penguins require a lot of food for their enormous chicks, preying on deep-dwelling lanternfish especially.

The fish that little penguins chase typically occur within 30 metres of the surface; krill, squid and lanternfish may be hundreds of metres deeper. Which brings us back to body size because, if you remember, how deep a penguin can dive depends on its oxygen stores, which in turn depend on size (see p. 12).

Diving

Until about 30 years ago, what penguins did once they left the land was pretty much a mystery. Then the electronics revolution that brought us computers smaller than a house also brought us miniaturised devices that allowed us to spy on the penguins wherever they might go.

The real breakthrough to measure the diving behaviour of penguins was the development of the electronic time-depth recorder. This regularly measured the

An emperor penguin momentarily flies through the air as it exits the water.

depth a penguin was at, and recorded the data on a computer chip in a sealed block of waterproof resin glued or taped to the feathers.

The results were astonishing. First, it was discovered that penguins could dive to quite remarkable depths. All except the little penguin can easily go down beyond 100 metres – and do it over and over again. When feeding they may hold their breath for 3 minutes or more, or up to 10 minutes in the case of emperors. In fact emperors – the biggest penguins of all, remember – have been known to dive deeper than 600 metres, and the large males dive repeatedly to 500 metres when feeding. Try that with wings and see how far you get!

There is no doubt that by becoming flightless, the penguins opened up vast regions under the ocean that were previously unavailable to any bird. But there was a catch. Being able to dive and catch the fish is one thing; getting out to where the fish live is quite another. Getting out easily to their food is one advantage that flying seabirds enjoy – albatrosses, gannets: you name it. Swimming just is not as efficient or as fast as flying.

Swimming

Most penguins swim at a speed of around 2 metres per second. The small ones are a bit slower; emperors and kings a bit faster. It's not just slower than flying: it's *much* slower. So penguins must reach a workable compromise between the distance they must swim to their food and how long they can afford to be away from their nests.

No animal wants to travel any further than it needs to feed. The ideal for a penguin is for sufficient food to be available close to the colony, in a predictably sustainable manner, throughout the whole year. Such conditions are most likely to occur in the more tropical latitudes, where seasonal changes are much less marked than in the deep south.

There are some major basic differences of food supply between low and high latitudes, and between inshore and offshore feeding grounds. The offshore feeders fare better than inshore feeders if they are prepared to travel to areas of upwelling (where two bodies of water meet), because the upwelling stirs up nutrients that favour the growth of plankton. When upwelling is also combined with the long daylength of summer season at polar latitudes, there is a dramatic, albeit brief, flourishing of tiny plant and animal life that drives a 'bloom' of food for the penguins. It really is a case of 'making hay while the sun shines' for the southern penguins. The downside is that travelling several hundred kilometres to reach such rich feeding grounds means they have to be away from the nest for weeks at a time.

What tends to happen at higher latitudes is that, as the summer progresses, the bloom of food spreads into areas closer to the colonies, so that once the chicks hatch they can be fed more easily and frequently. In fact, while daylength tells penguins when it's time for breeding, in the long run it is natural selection that determines when they start breeding, as this ensures the peak feeding demand of chicks coincides with the maximum local availability of food. The upside of all this is that offshore-feeding parents can feed their chicks more when it matters most, so they grow faster. Chicks of offshore-feeding parents typically fledge a month earlier than those of inshore-feeding penguins.

Snares penguins can dive repeatedly to depths of over 100 metres when feeding.

Royal penguins, a subspecies of macaroni penguins, make the transition from swimmer to walker.

The tyranny of distance

There is, however, a limit to how much food a foraging parent can bring back over a long distance. Inshore-feeding penguins, such as yellow-eyed penguins breeding on the Otago Peninsula, and little penguins at Oamaru, usually forage within 20 kilometres of the shore and typically try to rear two chicks. As the foraging distance increases, it becomes less likely that penguins will be able to provide enough food for two chicks. Adélie penguins may travel several hundred kilometres during incubation and more than 20 kilometres when rearing chicks; they are more likely to rear two chicks in years when the food supply is particularly good. Crested penguins travel hundreds of kilometres during incubation and more than 100 kilometres while feeding the chick, but while they lay two eggs, they only ever rear one chick.

Emperor and king penguins travel the furthest from the colony and lay but a single egg – they don't even try to start with two. Kings are actually the kings in more ways than one: they travel the furthest of any penguin while feeding chicks. Their chicks are so large that they take more than a year to raise, which is very unusual for birds. During the winter months, parents leave their chicks alone in the colony while they travel for a month or more seeking food – and in some extreme cases the chicks may be left alone to fast for up to five and a half months.

Porpoising

Porpoising is a fast swimming method that penguins use when trying to escape a predator or travel quickly. As the name suggests, they move like porpoises and dolphins. It is not as efficient as swimming at a slow speed, but it's way faster.

Although penguins are well streamlined, as they attempt to push themselves faster through a dense medium like water, the amount of drag increases. At a certain speed, which for most moderately sized penguins is about 3 metres per second, it actually makes more sense to propel themselves out of the water and move through the air, which is much less resistant. It's also an opportunity to take a breath while on the run – or should that be on the fly? It's the closest penguins get to experiencing what their ancestors gave up 60 million years ago on the shores of a sinking continent called Zealandia.

Migration

Food at higher latitudes is seasonal and transitory, so offshore feeders must migrate to feed. It is the most dangerous time for penguins: sometimes up to a quarter of adult Adélies do not survive winter. It is even more dangerous for the fledgling chicks, more than half of which typically perish before they reach adulthood.

Adult inshore feeders have it easier, for although their food at low latitudes is less plentiful, it tends to be available year-round, so there is no need to migrate. Even so, when confronted by a dwindling food supply, such as in an El Niño year, inshore-feeding penguins are flexible enough to journey further afield.

Tracking penguins with radio transmitters, satellite transmitters and GPS loggers is starting to show us some amazing things. Yellow-eyed penguins breeding near Oamaru follow underwater 'highways', making turns at precise locations that correspond to underwater ridges or reefs. But it would be wrong to assume that this is the norm: most penguins seem remarkably varied and flexible in their at-sea behaviour. We still have much to learn about how penguins find their way around.

Penguins undergo some quite incredible migrations for any bird, flying or not. Some Adélie penguins that breed on Ross Island manage a round-trip of about 6000 kilometres every winter as they journey north to feed in the Southern Ocean.

Typically the least social of penguins, yellow-eyed penguins will congregate as they exit the water.

We really have no idea where erect-crested, Fiordland and Snares penguins go during the off-season, but it is likely to be far from their colonies. Now that we have the technology, hopefully the answers to some of those questions may appear in the near future.

It is when juvenile birds fledge that they undertake the greatest migrations. With the exception of little penguins, which can return to breed as one-year-olds, other young penguins typically spend two or more years away 'earning their stripes' before they have the temerity to try breeding. It's as if evolution sets the same question year after year: 'Welcome to the world of water; now can you figure it out? If you do, we'll take the best of you back.'

PREDATORS AT SEA

Seals are in many respects the mammalian equivalent of penguins: warm-blooded creatures that evolved into the ocean and now must balance their lives between breeding on land and feeding at sea. But if penguins expected sympathy from seals, they were mistaken. Seals are an adult penguin's worst enemy. Leopard seals, in particular, make a habit of hanging about penguin colonies – especially those of Adélie penguins and the other members of the genus *Pygoscelis* in Antarctica – hoping to catch a penguin as it enters or leaves the water. At one Adélie penguin colony on Ross Island it was estimated that leopard seals took up to 1 per cent of the breeding adult penguins during the season, although it varies a lot from one year to the next. When they do catch a penguin, leopard seals play with it like a cat with a mouse, letting it go then catching it again, often diving with it (possibly to drown the penguin), and slapping the penguin's body on the sea's surface (to skin it).

Leopard seals extend up into the sub-Antarctic, and the odd one shows up on beaches around Otago, in the sub-Antarctic and on the south-eastern coast of the New Zealand mainland.

Hooker's sea lions also hunt and kill penguins, and on the Antipodes Islands, male New Zealand fur seals have been observed running down erect-crested penguins on the rocks before killing and eating them. Even a seal as seemingly awkward and docile as a Weddell seal may occasionally prey on penguins in Antarctica.

The penguins' main defence when in the water is their agility and speed. Killer whales are known to target emperor and king penguins, but they seem not to bother with the smaller penguins except the occasional Adélie. Sharks, too, tackle penguins on occasion. Around New Zealand it is not uncommon to find penguins with wounds from sharks, especially those that have lost a foot – perhaps bitten off when the penguin was sleeping at sea?

CONSERVATION AND EXPLOITATION

Even penguins as isolated as king penguins are never far from the footprint of humans.

Sixty-odd million years ago, after primordial penguins made the transition from flying in the air to diving in the sea, *Waimanu* and all the penguins that followed could never evolve wings again. And for millions of years that didn't matter much. The ledger sheet still favoured the underwater diver; the gains outweighed the losses.

Then humans came along and spoiled everything. About ten thousand years ago, they started agriculture, domestication and the whole train of events that would affect all the things in their environment. Even the most isolated of penguins have not been able to avoid troubles at the hand of humans, which have been truly exacerbated by the birds' inability to fly.

For penguins in the New Zealand region, none of that mattered too much until 600–700 years ago when the first humans made it to our shores. In the sub-Antarctic islands it was later still, when 200 years ago whalers and sealers arrived and started taking penguins too, especially once the bigger animals became depleted. In the Ross Sea sector of Antarctica, it's been barely a hundred years, with the main human intrusion in the 50-year span following the International Geophysical Year in 1957–58, which launched the first co-ordinated scientific assault on Antarctica.

Exploitation

A plump bird that could only waddle when on land must have been easy pickings for all hungry humans. To a certain extent they were: penguins have been found at Maori midden sites (rubbish dumps near where food had been prepared and cooked) in both the North and South Islands. Recent evidence suggests that Maori may have been responsible for the extermination of a penguin species closely related to yellow-eyed penguins (see panel overleaf). Fortunately for penguins, apparently they are not exactly the tastiest of meats. However, their high oil content means they can still be useful.

Joseph Hatch and the penguins of Macquarie

If Australia usurped our right to Macquarie Island and its penguins by putting politics before geography, one New Zealander did virtually all he could to claim the penguins back ... but just for his own profit.

Joseph Hatch was the mayor of Invercargill, the local member of parliament, and an entrepreneur. He saw an opportunity at Macquarie Island for boiling down elephant seals to make oil, which was needed for making ropes (an essential item of industry in those days). He subsequently realised that the island's millions of penguins would be a lot easier to catch than the elephant seals. He set up a factory on Macquarie, and in 20 years from 1889 it is said that his men boiled up three million penguins (mainly king penguins) for their oil.

In the end, it was Australia's Antarctic hero, Douglas Mawson, who led the fight to have Hatch stopped. So, while Macquarie's penguins should perhaps belong to New Zealand, it is a bitter truth that their welfare has been better served under the Australian flag.

MURDER OF THE *MEGADYPTES*?

The yellow-eyed penguin is the sole survivor of the genus *Megadyptes*. While the Auckland and Campbell Islands are its current strongholds, the few yellow-eyed penguins breeding on Stewart Island and the south-eastern coast of the South Island have long been regarded as remnants of a larger population that stretched right up the South Island and possibly into the North Island. This conclusion was based largely on sub-fossil bones uncovered from Maori midden sites. It is thought that first the Maori ate them, and then European farmers cleared their habitat and introduced predatory mammals.

Recent re-examination of the bones extracted from the middens, which had been classified as belonging to yellow-eyed penguins, showed that they were smaller than present-day yellow-eyed penguins. DNA extracted from the bones suggested that they were another species of the genus *Megadyptes*, distinct from yellow-eyed penguins.

History has been rewritten. Now the story goes like this. Following the arrival of Maori migrants, the small *Megadyptes* penguins were eaten and eventually exterminated. About 500 years ago, yellow-eyed penguins from the sub-Antarctic islands were able to establish a breeding presence on the south-eastern corner of the South Island in the absence of their erstwhile competitors.

The penguin supposedly eaten to extinction is tentatively called *Megadyptes waitaha* after the Maori tribe that first settled the South Island.

Introduced predators

It was always a fair bet that humans could find many more ways to kill penguins than just boiling them. Perhaps the most deadly has been the introduction of foreign predators. Maori and, later, European settlers brought with them predators from faraway places – rats, dogs, cats, pigs, stoats and ferrets. The kiwi, the kakapo and the penguin were sitting ducks.

Autopsies of little penguins found dead around North Otago in recent times showed one in six had been killed by dogs. On the Otago Peninsula and further south in the Catlins, stoats and ferrets, which most of the year prey on rabbits, find yellow-eyed penguin chicks to be easy pickings. Probably the only reason yellow-eyed penguins remain on the mainland is the concerted efforts of the Department of Conservation and the Yellow-eyed Penguin Trust, which trap and kill predators near penguin colonies. Such a marriage of convenience between humans and penguins needs to be a lifelong commitment – not just 'lifelong' in human terms, but for the life of the species. In other words, forever or until extinction do us part.

On the sub-Antarctic islands, whalers and sealers introduced rats and cats. In addition to the damage such animals can inflict directly on the penguins, they carry ticks, fleas and lice which are vectors of diseases that can kill penguins and their chicks.

Feral cats are one of a number of introduced predators that prey on little penguins.

Clearing the land for farming has decimated the breeding habitat of the forest-dwelling yellow-eyed penguin.

Disease

Relatively little is known of the diseases that affect penguins. During the 1990s a mystery illness killed many yellow-eyed penguins breeding on the Otago Peninsula. Avian malaria was implicated, and it is certainly true that antibodies for avian malaria can be found in the blood of many penguins.

A viral disease found in domestic chickens was the chief suspect in the mass deaths of Adélie penguin chicks in Antarctica in the 1970s. It is thought that the pathogen could have been introduced in chicken meat taken there to feed humans and then spread by scavenging skuas. Consequently, many Antarctic research programmes, including the New Zealand one, now ban chicken products.

Habitat destruction and farming

On the New Zealand mainland, probably nothing has done more to wipe out penguins from certain areas than the rape and pillage of the land in the name of farming. The destruction of coastal forest has robbed the yellow-eyed penguin of much of its former mainland distribution. Replanting programmes in isolated pockets on the Otago and Southland coasts have met with some success, but the yellow-eyed penguin remains one of the rarest in the world.

New Zealand is often touted as 'a nation of sheep' but it should be remembered that, for more than 60 million years, we were a nation of penguins.

Climate change and El Niño

New Zealand has its 'clean, green' image and indeed its penguins face less risk from pollution, overfishing of their prey, mortality due to by-catch, habitat destruction and direct exploitation of their eggs than they do in some other parts of the southern hemisphere. Yet it would be naive to imagine that our penguins are immune to human-induced environmental changes.

Perhaps the most insidious threat is global warming. Penguins have always been sensitive to changes that affect their food supply: for example, sea-surface temperature which affects the mixing of water and nutrients responsible for the 'bloom' of productivity that fuels breeding. There are naturally occurring rhythms in large-scale climatic variables that cause regular change at the local level, and for millennia penguins have evolved to cope with variation in their environment, such as those resulting from the predictable patterns of El Niño and La Niña. But over the last 50 years or so, the world's temperature has been rising, affecting food availability over and above the normal natural oscillations. Rising sea surface temperatures associated

Populations of rockhopper penguins have been severely impacted by aspects of climate change such as increasing sea surface temperatures.

with global warming were implicated in the massive decline that has occurred in the numbers of rockhopper penguins breeding on Campbell Island. Warmer water may also result in algal blooms that can produce biotoxins fatal for penguins, such as those suspected of killing yellow-eyed penguins in Otago during 1990.

Tourism

Tourism makes penguins economically valuable, enhancing prospects of their being conserved. It also creates ambassadors for the penguins: people who have seen penguins in the wild are more likely to become advocates for their preservation.

However, a balance needs to be struck between giving the public access to the penguins and protecting them from intrusions that harm them or reduce their prospects of breeding successfully.

It does seem from managed penguin tourism operations in other parts of the world, such as those at Punta Tombo in Argentina and Phillip Island in Australia, that penguins have an amazing capacity to get used to humans if access is controlled and limited by pathways and fences. Healthy tourism is the kind that puts the humans in the cage and leaves the penguins in the wild.

Fiordland penguins face potential threats from tourism, which paradoxically also offers the prospect of salvation.

Places to see penguins

The best place to see little penguins is at the Oamaru Blue Penguin Colony (www.penguins.co.nz), where more than two hundred penguins come ashore each evening during the peak of the breeding season. For yellow-eyed penguins, the Otago Peninsula and the Catlins offer the best viewing, with the Department of Conservation's hide at Sandfly Bay (www.doc.govt.nz) a great vantage point to watch them coming ashore in the late afternoon. There are also two commercial operations run by Penguin Place (www.penguinplace.co.nz) and Elm Wildlife Tours (www.elmwildlifetours.co.nz). Fiordland penguins tend to be especially shy but there are several places on the Fiordland coast, plus Jacksons Bay in South Westland, where they can be seen by those prepared to do some walking first (www.doc.govt.nz).

Access to penguins on the sub-Antarctic islands and the Ross Sea sector of Antarctica is best gained through cruise ships, such as those run by Heritage Expeditions (www.heritage-expeditions.com).

Tourists encounter gentoo penguins: keeping their distance, taking only photos, and leaving with a will to help conserve them.

It is important not to disturb penguins when viewing them in the wild. Even if penguins on nests do not run away, the mere presence of humans can cause them stress such as elevated heart rates and energy consumption. Where possible, tourists should use hides (these are often provided at public viewing sites) or seek cover behind sand dunes and vegetation. Never go closer than 10 metres, keep low to the ground, and be as quiet and still as possible. Keep children under control. Never take animals with you. Take photographs, but do not use a flash. If you do all that, not only is your encounter likely to be less stressful for the penguin, it's likely to be more rewarding for you.

One final note: when penguins moult they must replace their feather survival suits with new feathers. The process takes 2–3 weeks and, without the insulation and waterproofing necessary to stay in water, moulting penguins are forced to fast on land. During this period, they conserve energy by standing very still and, as the new feathers push out the old ones, they can look decidedly scruffy. Many tourists mistakenly assume moulting penguins are sick. They are not – and the best you can do for them is to leave them in peace.

Above and right: King penguins. Penguins are to birds what seals are to mammals: creatures that went back to the ocean but which are tied to the land for breeding.

Penguins in captivity

Penguins in zoos can make for a sad sight, especially if their surroundings are unsympathetic to their needs. Worldwide there are hundreds of zoos with penguins. But the news is not all bad. For some species, like the endangered Galápagos penguin, captive breeding programmes may offer their only hope of avoiding extinction. Sea World in San Diego pioneered the keeping of penguins under conditions that mimic those found in their natural environment and, as a consequence, have been very successful at breeding penguins. There were a few hiccups, like the time they removed 60 emperor penguins from the colony at Cape Crozier on Ross Island (about a fifth of the colony) only to lose them in a fire when a refrigeration unit malfunctioned.

In New Zealand, king and gentoo penguins can be seen under such naturalistic conditions at Kelly Tarlton's in Auckland (www.kellytarltons.co.nz) where each day they make three tonnes of snow for the penguin enclosure. Thanks to the success of Sea World's breeding programme, the exhibit was able to be stocked with penguins that were themselves hatched in captivity. The temperature and lighting regimes at Kelly Tarlton's are varied as they would be in the wild, and this has encouraged their penguins to breed too.

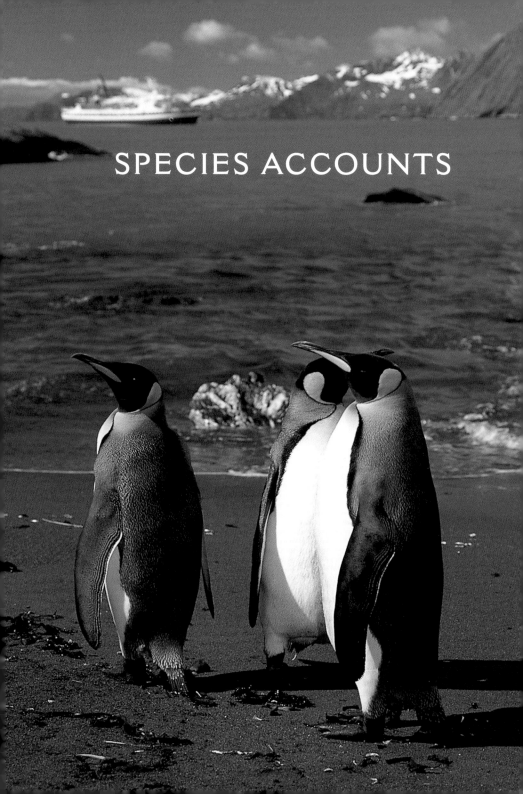

SPECIES ACCOUNTS

Little penguin

Scientific name: *Eudyptula minor*
Maori name: Korora

Also known as the blue penguin, the little blue penguin and, in Australia, the fairy penguin. Since it is the world's smallest penguin, the name 'little penguin' seems apt; also it is the name that was standardised at the 2nd International Penguin Conference held in Australia in 1992.

Identification: Weighing only 1 kg or so and 40–45 cm in length, little penguins sport bluish plumage on their upper parts, hence their alternative names. The back can be pale blue to a dark grey-blue depending upon age, season or subspecies. When on land they distinctly lean forwards, in contrast to the more upright stance of other penguins. They're also largely nocturnal, coming ashore after sunset.

The little penguin closely resembles juveniles of the genus *Spheniscus,* but their geographic ranges do not overlap so they are unlikely to be confused in the wild.

Distribution: North Island, South Island, Stewart Island and Chatham Islands. In Australia, from Western Australia along the southern coast and up to New South Wales. Between different areas they vary considerably in size, the amount of white on the tail and flipper, and the colour tone of the back.

Six subspecies are recognised: *novaehollandiae* in Australia, *iredalei* in northern New Zealand, *variabilis* in the Cook Strait region, *albosignata* on Banks Peninsula and Motunau Island, *minor* in the lower part of the South Island, and *chathamensis* at the Chatham Islands. Some have argued that the white-flippered penguin (*Eudyptula minor albosignata*), found mainly on Banks Peninsula and Motunau Island, is a separate species. It freely interbreeds, however, with other subspecies, and molecular studies demonstrate that it is part of a genetic grouping with three of the other little penguin subspecies. Interestingly, the southernmost subspecies (*minor*) and the Australian subspecies (*novaehollandiae*) are closer to each other genetically (despite the wide expanse of ocean between them) than they are to the other four subspecies.

Habitat: Little penguins nest in burrows, caves, rock crevices, and sometimes under bushes and trees. They are nocturnal on land, typically coming ashore after dusk and leaving before dawn. Their nests tend to be clustered to form colonies. When at sea, little penguins tend to stay close to the coast.

Length and height are not the same thing with a penguin. This is because the bird is stretched out longer when it's swimming but has a shorter posture when standing. The length describes the measurement from the tips of the toes to the tip of the bill when the bird is stretched out. The tallest penguin, the emperor, is 115 cm in length but stands typically about 1 metre tall.

Breeding: The season begins any time from late June to September. There is no clearly defined period of arrival, with individuals continuing to visit the colony outside of the breeding season. Usually they lay a clutch of two eggs 3 days apart and incubate for 33–37 days. In some places, e.g. Oamaru and the Otago Peninsula, double-brooding may occur whereby a second clutch is laid in a single breeding season after the first chicks have fledged.

For the most part, little penguins behave like inshore foragers, with feeding trips lasting less than a day during incubation and chick-rearing. However, in some places, e.g. the Marlborough Sounds, feeding trips of a week or more during the incubation period are not uncommon. Chicks are guarded by their parents usually for 20–30 days, but sometimes as few as 8 days. Chicks of cave-dwelling little penguins, such as those on Banks Peninsula, may form small crèches. Fledging takes 48–63 days.

Diet: Little penguins feed mainly on fish, especially sardines (pilchards) and anchovies, but also squid and occasionally crustaceans.

Migration: Juveniles disperse widely after fledging. In Australia, adults sometimes undertake long trips at sea during the non-breeding season, but return regularly to the colony throughout the year.

Conservation: Categorised by the IUCN (International Union for Conservation of Nature) as being of 'lower risk'. Not globally threatened. Total population estimated at about a million birds, of which about half may be breeders, i.e. around 250,000 pairs. The population of the white-flippered subspecies, *E. m. albosignata*, consists of about 2200 pairs and is listed as 'endangered'.

Yellow-eyed penguin

Scientific name: *Megadyptes antipodes*
Maori name: Hoiho

Though rare and with the likelihood of extinction lingering not too far away, the yellow-eyed penguin is nevertheless among the most accessible of New Zealand penguins. It can be seen readily on the Otago Peninsula and other places on the south-eastern coast of the South Island.

Identification: A medium-sized penguin, up to 76 cm long and 5.5 kg. Recognisable by its yellow eyes and stripes of yellow feathers that extend back from the eyes to join behind the head. Moulting birds and birds at sea may be confused with crested penguins. Immature birds are similar to adults but have a pale yellow chin and a less vivid yellow eye-stripe.

Distribution: Endemic to New Zealand, and mainly found on the Auckland and Campbell Islands, where more than a thousand breed at each locality. On the mainland, they breed along the south-eastern coast of the South Island, from Oamaru south to Foveaux Strait and the nearby islands, including Stewart Island and Codfish Island (Whenua Hou). Another small isolated group breeds on Banks Peninsula.

Habitat: The yellow-eyed is an unusual penguin in many respects. It nests under dense vegetation – usually in forest – for protection from the sun, and is the least social of all penguins, with nests often tens or hundreds of metres apart. This dependence on vegetative cover has made them particularly vulnerable on the New Zealand mainland, where farming has cleared much of the forest. At sea, they tend to be found in pairs or alone.

Breeding: Usually two similar-sized eggs are laid in September/October. Both parents alternate nest attendance every day or two during incubation, which is quite variable (39–51 days). Chicks are guarded by a parent for the first 40–50 days of their lives; they rarely form crèches. Hatching is synchronous within a brood, with chicks in nearly two-thirds of nests hatching on the same day as their sibling. Chicks do not fledge until about 106 days old.

Diet: Yellow-eyed penguins feed mainly on fish. They are often described as benthic (sea-bottom) feeders – but like all penguins are in fact opportunistic feeders that will take fish in open water too. Normally they eat just a few squid, but these become more important as food when fish numbers are low.

Migration: Resident (non-migratory). Adults can be found near the breeding colonies throughout the year. Juveniles disperse around New Zealand.

Conservation: Classified as 'vulnerable'. Population estimates put the total number of yellow-eyed penguins in the world at 5000–7000 birds, including about 2000 breeding pairs. On the Otago Peninsula, numbers have fluctuated dramatically in recent times, illustrating both human interference and the vulnerability of inshore-feeding penguins to changing local conditions. Yellow-eyed penguins are often cited as the world's rarest species, but that dubious distinction probably belongs now to the even more endangered Galápagos penguin.

Fiordland penguin

Scientific name: *Eudyptes pachyrhynchus*
Maori name: Tawaki

Also known as the Fiordland crested penguin. Somewhat incongruously, these penguins breed in the rainforest of the South Island's south-west coast.

Identification: Around 67 cm long and weighing about 4 kg, with a thick yellow stripe running above the eye and ending in a drooping plume. Very similar to Snares penguin, but can be distinguished by its larger size, a series of white streaks on the cheeks (most apparent when a bird is excited) and the lack of a fleshy margin at the base of the bill. Immature birds have a mottled white chin and thinner, dull yellow plumes, and cannot be easily distinguished from immature Snares penguins.

Distribution: Endemic to New Zealand: the south-western coast of the South Island, Stewart Island and associated offshore islands.

Habitat: Fiordland penguins breed under high rainforest canopy, in dense shrub, under boulders and in caves. Nests are lined with twigs and grass. Colonies usually consist of loose groups that contain from a few to tens of nests, and nests can be several metres apart. All breeding grounds are both near to and north of the Subtropical Convergence, an oceanic front that likely provides food for the breeding birds, even in winter.

Breeding: The breeding season begins in June/July, during the southern winter. Males arrive before females. They fast for 40–45 days from arrival until their first foraging trip. A clutch of two different-sized eggs is laid, the larger, second egg 4 days after the first. Both sexes share incubation for the first 5–10 days. Unlike other crested penguins, it is typically the female that takes the first foraging trip, of 13 days, with males subsequently being away for a similar period. The incubation period for second eggs is 32 days, and this egg hatches several days before the first one. The smaller chick from the first egg usually dies within a few days, from starvation. Chicks start to form crèches at 2–3 weeks and fledge at about 75 days.

Diet: In one study on the west coast of the South Island, squid made up over 80 per cent of the diet, the rest being crustaceans and fish. However, depending upon the time and place, fish may assume greater importance in the diet.

Migration: Fiordland penguins migrate into the Tasman Sea, as indicated by at-sea observations and the occurrence of moulting birds in eastern Australia. Birds regularly moult on the Snares Islands. Vagrants have been recorded on the Chathams, Campbell and Macquarie Islands, and from as far afield as Western Australia.

Conservation: Listed as 'vulnerable'. Population estimates are 2500–3000 nests, which is a rough guide to the number of breeding pairs. The population appears to have declined over the past hundred years, with recent local declines apparent in some localities.

Snares penguin

Scientific name: *Eudyptes robustus*
Maori name: Tawaki

Also known as the Snares crested penguin. Snares penguins have the good fortune to live in one of the most pristine, predator-free and least disturbed places possible: the Snares Islands, where the Department of Conservation tightly restricts access. Nevertheless, Snares penguins are regarded as 'vulnerable' owing to their confined distribution.

Identification: Like a slightly smaller version of the Fiordland penguin, at 65 cm length and roughly 3 kg, they are distinguished by having a fleshy margin at the base of the bill. They differ from erect-crested penguins in having drooping feather plumes on the crest and a more conical bill, and the yellow facial stripe reaches further up the bill.

Distribution: Endemic to the Snares Islands, about 100 km south of Stewart Island. With a breeding range confined to just over 300 ha, they have the most restricted distribution of all penguins. Little is known about how widely they range outside of the breeding season.

Habitat: Snares penguins nest in dense colonies, building cup-shaped nests using peat, wood and pebbles. They breed under the canopy of *Olearia* forests and on exposed coastal rock. The forest in and around a colony is often killed by penguin guano, creating clearings in the forest.

Breeding: They arrive at the colony in August/September, and lay eggs in September/October. They have to go without food for 37–39 days from arrival until their first feeding trip. Two different-sized eggs are laid 4–5 days apart. The incubation period is 33 days and, like Fiordland penguins, only the first-hatched chick, from the second-laid egg, usually survives beyond the first few days. Chicks form crèches at about 33 days, and fledge at about three and a half months.

Diet: The little information that is available indicates that this species lives mainly on krill, squid and fish.

Migration: Thought to move westwards into the Tasman Sea. Vagrants have been recorded on Macquarie Island and on the Falkland Islands.

Conservation: Even though the population is stable or increasing at about 30,000 pairs, Snares penguins are classified by the IUCN as 'vulnerable' because their breeding is confined to such a small area, making them susceptible to local changes in the environment.

Erect-crested penguin

Scientific name: *Eudyptes sclateri*

This has been referred to as 'the last penguin', in the sense that it is the least-studied and least-known of all the living penguins, primarily because it breeds in such isolated places.

Identification: A relatively solid, medium-sized penguin at 68 cm in length and 5–6 kg, with strikingly upright yellow plumes when it is dry on land. Similar in appearance to other crested penguins, in particular Snares and Fiordland penguins, but the yellow stripe attaches higher on the bill than in the other two species. Identification at sea is extremely difficult because the feather plumes droop down when wet. Immature erect-crested penguins have a pale yellow stripe, no long plumes, and a mottled grey throat.

Distribution: Largely restricted to the Antipodes and Bounty Islands, with a few isolated pairs breeding on the Auckland Islands. Until recently there were also some breeding on Campbell Island. Sub-fossil remains have also been found on the Chatham Islands.

Habitat: Erect-crested penguins breed in dense colonies on rocky slopes and platforms bordering the shore. A few build nests but most lay their eggs directly onto the bare rock.

Breeding: Birds arrive at the colony in September. After a long period establishing a nest site, attracting a mate and then undergoing courtship (up to 3 weeks), they lay two eggs. The first, much smaller egg is invariably lost, in most cases on the same day or before the second egg has been laid. Egg size differences are extreme, with the first egg averaging only 82 g compared with 151 g for the second egg. The laying interval is 5 days, with incubation lasting about 35 days. Chicks begin crèching at about 21 days and are fledged at around 75–90 days.

Diet: Diet has not been studied in this species, but birds probably travel to oceanic frontal zones and take advantage of the high productivity there, feeding mainly on pelagic crustaceans, fish and squid.

Migration: The winter distribution of erect-crested penguins at sea is unknown. Some moult regularly on other sub-Antarctic Islands south of New Zealand and, less commonly, on the South Island. Vagrants have been recorded in Northland, Tasmania, southern Australia, Heard Island and the Falkland Islands.

Conservation: Categorised as 'endangered'. While available estimates put the total population at 165,000–175,000 pairs, this is likely to be an overestimate. More recent sampling suggests significant declines (with one extrapolation concluding there may be fewer than 30,000 pairs), in line with substantial reductions that have been observed at the Antipodes and a former breeding site, Campbell Island, over more than three decades.

Rockhopper penguin

Scientific name: *Eudyptes chrysocome*

These are small penguins which, with the wild plumes that emanate from above their eyes, look as though they are always having a 'bad hair day'.

Identification: The smallest of the crested penguins, at 61 cm in length and about 2.5 kg, rockhoppers are also distinguished from other crested penguins by having only a thin yellow stripe above the eyes that ends in a wild collection of drooping plumes. They also have distinctive red eyes. They are currently regarded as three subspecies, but it seems likely that at least one of them, the northern rockhopper or Moseley's penguin (*Eudyptes chrysocome moseleyi*), is a separate species. The other two subspecies are the southern rockhopper *E. c. filholi* (found in the New Zealand sub-Antarctic islands) and *E. c. chrysocome* (found in South America and the Falkland Islands). The crests of southern rockhopper penguins differ from their northern counterparts in having shorter plumes. Their vocalisations are also different. Immature birds have a narrow yellow stripe and a pale mottled grey chin. Juvenile southern and northern rockhopper penguins are almost impossible to tell apart.

Distribution: Breeds in the sub-Antarctic, with a circumpolar distribution including Campbell, Auckland and Antipodes Islands.

Habitat: Breeding colonies are located on rocky slopes and among tussocks, sometimes in small caves or crevices. A small nest is build from tussock, peat and pebbles.

Breeding: Southern rockhoppers start arriving to breed in October/November. Males arrive about a week before females. A clutch of two different-sized eggs is laid 4–5 days apart. Male and female remain at the nest sharing incubation for the first 12 days or so; thereafter the male takes the first foraging trip and the female the next, each of which lasts nearly 2 weeks. In all, males fast for 33 days from arrival, whereas females fast for 39 days. Most of the first-laid eggs are lost during incubation, which takes about 34 days. The few chicks that hatch from first-laid eggs almost invariably die within the first few days. The guard stage lasts for 20–26 days and the birds fledge at 66–73 days.

Diet: Most studies of this species show crustaceans, especially krill, are the main food. Fish and squid play a minor role.

Migration: The non-breeding range of rockhopper penguins is poorly known. Moulting birds have been found in South Africa, Australia and New Zealand. Vagrant northern rockhoppers have been recorded on the Chatham Islands.

Conservation: All three subspecies are classified as 'vulnerable'. The total population is estimated at about 2,000,000 pairs, but substantial declines have occurred over most of their distribution in recent years.

Adélie penguin

Scientific name: *Pygoscelis adeliae*

The French explorer Dumont D'Urville lent his wife's name (Adélie) to this penguin when he encountered it in the Antarctic.

Identification: About 71 cm in length and 5 kg in weight, this is the classic 'tuxedoed' black-and-white penguin of cartoons, readily identifiable by the white eye-ring and feathers extending along the bill. Feathers on the back of the head are slightly elongated and can be raised to form a small crest when aroused. A few birds (about one in 100,000) have a genetic mutation that causes the normally black feathers to be white to yellow, or even brown. Immature birds up to 14 months of age have a white rather than black chin and lack the white ring around the eyes.

Distribution: Circumpolar distribution, confined to the Antarctic where they breed on the shores of the continent and off-lying islands. There are six breeding colonies on Ross Island, and others north along the western coastline of the Ross Sea to Cape Adare, which has the largest Adélie penguin colony in the world. They have the distinction of breeding further south than any other penguin (indeed, any other bird), with the colony at Cape Royds, Ross Island, being at latitude 77°33'S.

Habitat: Adélie penguins breed in colonies ranging from a few individuals to many thousands. Within the colonies, discrete sub-colonies form, with the land in between free of nests. The penguins prefer to nest on ridges and other areas from which the snow melts away first. The nests themselves are depressions or scrapes in the ground, which the penguins line with small stones. The stones help to keep eggs out of any meltwater from snow and are often in short supply so there may be intense competition for them: many Adélies steal stones from their neighbours' nests. The availability of accessible ice-free nesting habitats probably limits the distribution of this species, such as along the coastline of the Ross Sea. Adélies are highly gregarious, both on land and at sea.

Breeding: Birds start to arrive at the colony in October, with the timing of breeding being somewhat later the further south one goes. Males tend to arrive slightly before females. From arrival to egg-laying takes about 12 days at colonies on Ross Island. A clutch of two eggs is laid, typically 3 days apart. At Cape Bird, on Ross Island, the first eggs of the season are almost consistently laid on 4 November, give or take only a day or so. Laying is highly synchronous, with two-thirds of clutches being started within a 6-day period. The male takes the first incubation shift, of 11–17 days depending upon locality and year, and this is followed by an 11- to 13-day shift by the female. The third shift, taken by the male, tends to be about 5 days or less. The incubation period is 35 days for first eggs and 33–34 days for second eggs. Chicks are guarded for an average of 22 days, although this varies from 17 to 30 days. Fledging occurs at 48–51 days on Ross Island, but takes longer (60–61 days) near the northern limits of their distribution.

Diet: Adélie penguins feed mainly on krill. The Ross Island colonies tend to take mainly the smaller krill species, *Euphausia crystallorophias*, while elsewhere the main food is the larger krill, *E. superba*. Fish and amphipods can be common in the diet of Ross Island birds.

Migration: Adélie penguins are migratory and after breeding do not return to their colonies until the next spring. Satellite telemetry indicates that Adélie penguins from the Ross Sea leave this area in autumn, with some migrating to an area west of the Balleny Islands and others migrating in a north-easterly direction. Juveniles are suspected to travel even further north than adults. Vagrant birds have been recorded as far north as Macquarie Island, Tasmania and the South Island.

Conservation: Considered of 'lower risk' because the population is stable and not globally threatened. Population estimated at about 2,500,000 pairs including over 600,000 pairs in the Ross Sea sector of Antarctica.

Chinstrap penguin

Scientific name: *Pygoscelis antarctica*

One of the most striking penguins to look at, this is one seldom seen in New Zealand waters because in this part of its range it breeds at one of the most out-of-the-way places possible: the Balleny Islands.

Identification: Medium-sized, at about 77 cm long and 4–5 kg, and readily recognisable by the white face and fine black line across the cheeks. The demarcation between the black and white lies above the eye, isolating the dark eye in the white plumage. The bill is black. Unlike most other penguins, juvenile chinstraps closely resemble their parents. Until their first moult, they can be recognised by dark spotting around the eyes and a slightly shorter bill.

Distribution: Mostly concentrated around the Antarctic Peninsula, but a few breed on the Balleny Islands, near the Ross Sea.

Habitat: Usually breeds on hillside slopes and rocky outcrops in colonies that sometimes can be enormous. At the South Shetland Islands, chinstrap penguins often breed among other *Pygoscelis* penguins, though usually on steeper slopes.

Breeding: Arrive in colonies October/November, and lay eggs in November/December. Females may arrive on average 5 days later than their male partners. Both fast at the colony for about 2–3 weeks before laying a clutch of usually two eggs, 3 days apart. Females most often take the first incubation shift, and the first four shifts are 5–10 days each. Incubation averages 36 days for first eggs and 34 days for second eggs. Chicks crèche at 23–29 days and fledge at 52–60 days.

Diet: Chinstrap penguins feed almost exclusively on krill (*Euphausia superba*). Other crustaceans and fish play a minor role.

Migration: Chinstrap penguins leave their breeding colonies during winter and probably migrate north of the pack-ice, staying at sea until the next spring. Non-breeders have been recorded in other parts of Antarctica, such as Adélie Land, and some have been known to journey as far afield as Australia and Tierra del Fuego.

Conservation: Listed as of 'lower risk', like the Adélies, chinstraps have a stable population that is not globally threatened. The total population is estimated at 7,500,000 pairs, but fewer than 1500 pairs breed on the Balleny Islands.

Emperor penguin

Scientific name: *Aptenodytes forsteri*

Emperor penguins lay only a single egg, which is incubated on their feet rather than in a nest. The emperor penguin is a bird of extremes in just about every way. It is the biggest penguin and breeds during the Antarctic winter.

Identification: The largest of all living penguins, up to 115 cm in length and weighing 38 kg. Distinguished from the smaller king penguin by its size, more robust stature, and a broad pale yellow connection between the orange-yellow ear patches and the pale yellow upper breast. Immature birds resemble adults, but are smaller and have a white rather than black chin. Ear patches of juveniles are whitish, becoming increasingly yellow with age.

Distribution: Breeds exclusively in Antarctica and does so in the winter. Within the Ross Sea sector there are emperor penguin colonies at Cape Crozier on Ross Island, on Beaufort Island, and on the western shore of the Ross Sea at Cape Washington.

Habitat: Breeds during the Antarctic winter, from March to December, usually on fast ice. Probably depends a lot upon polynias (areas of open water surrounded by sea-ice) during winter. Eggs and chicks are balanced on the feet to prevent them from coming into contact with the ice. No nests are built, which allows the colony to move around and huddle close together, providing some protection from the cold.

Breeding: Birds arrive at the colony in March/April, and a single egg is laid in May/June. Males may arrive a few days before females. Females fast for about

40 days from arrival until the end of laying. Males incubate the egg on their feet for the entire incubation period of 62–67 days. Hence, from the time of arrival to the end of incubation, males must fast for about 115 days. Emperor penguins are colonial but not territorial, huddling together to withstand the cold and winds of the Antarctic winter. Chicks are guarded for about 45 days and fledge when about 5 months old.

Diet: Fish, squid and krill are taken to varying degrees, though squid and fish probably form the bulk of the diet.

Migration: Little is known about post-breeding dispersal or migration. Adults stay close to the permanent ice for most of their lives. Juveniles equipped with satellite transmitters, however, have been tracked as far north as the Polar Front. Vagrants have turned up on the South Shetland Islands, Tierra del Fuego, the Falklands, South Sandwich Islands, Kerguelen Island, Heard Island, and New Zealand.

Conservation: Like the other penguins that breed exclusively in Antarctica, emperor penguins are also categorised as 'lower risk'. Perhaps it is the isolation, but they too have a stable population that is not globally threatened. The population is estimated at about 218,000 pairs with one quarter of them breeding in the Ross Sea area.

Other penguins that visit the New Zealand region

King penguin

Scientific name: *Aptenodytes patagonicus*

The second-largest of the living penguins (94 cm, 14–16 kg), king penguins occur in a band around the sub-Antarctic, including Macquarie Island. They have orange ear patches and, apart from being smaller than the closely related emperor penguin, have greyish rather than black backs. They lay a single egg that they carry on their feet, but unlike emperors, they defend territories. Colonies can contain up to several hundred thousand individuals and are distinguished by having two cohorts of young. This comes about because king penguins take 14–16 months to rear their young, so at best can breed only twice every three years. They eat fish, in particular lanternfish, and in winter travel long distances in search of food. Vagrants have been observed on both islands of New Zealand and our sub-Antarctic islands. Classified as 'lower risk' with approximately 1,600,000 pairs in the world.

Magellanic penguin

Scientific name: *Spheniscus magellanicus*

The Magellanic penguin (71 cm, 4.5–5 kg) is distinguished from other *Spheniscus* penguins by having a second dark chest band and the least extensive areas of bare facial skin. Breeds around the bottom of South America: Argentina, Chile and the Falkland Islands. Magellanic penguins feed mainly on fish and, unlike the other members of their genus, are offshore feeders. Vagrants reach Australia and New Zealand; at 1.3 million pairs the species is considered of 'lower risk'.

Gentoo penguin

Scientific name: *Pygoscelis papua*

Similar in size to an Adélie penguin (76 cm, 5 kg), the gentoo penguin is distinguished by its orange-red bill and a patch of white that extends from both eyes and joins over the crown of the head. Found mainly in the sub-Antarctic, including Macquarie Island, gentoo penguins also breed on the Antarctic Peninsula. Inshore feeders, like yellow-eyed penguins, they prey on krill especially. Vagrants reach New Zealand, and the worldwide population of over 300,000 pairs is regarded as of 'lower risk'.

Macaroni penguin

Scientific name: *Eudyptes chrysolophus*

One of the crested penguins, the macaroni penguin (71 cm, 5 kg) is distinguished by its drooping orange plumes in contrast to the yellow crests of the other species. The species is found throughout the sub-Antarctic and on the Antarctic Peninsula; a white-faced subspecies breeds on Macquarie Island, where it is known as the royal penguin (*Eudyptes chrysolophus schlegeli*) and is given full species status by some authorities. The penguins on Macquarie feed mainly on krill and fish. Vagrants are sometimes found on the New Zealand mainland. Although macaroni penguins are probably the most numerous of all penguins, with a total population of some 10 million pairs (including nearly 1 million on Macquarie), the IUCN lists them as 'near threatened' (with the royal subspecies regarded as 'vulnerable') owing to substantial reductions in the population in parts of the species' range over the last three decades.

GLOSSARY

Throughout their range, rockhopper penguins are facing threats to their populations.

Bi-parental care: where both the male and female share the care and rearing of their eggs and chicks.

Brood patch: an area of bare skin infused with blood vessels that comes into contact with the eggs when being incubated and keeps them at close to the parent's body temperature.

Crèche: a congregation of three or more chicks in close proximity for protection from predators; during inclement weather, they may also huddle together for warmth.

Ecstatic display: a behavioural display performed by male penguins during courtship that is used to attract females. Typically includes repeated calling.

Guard stage: the initial period of chick development when a chick has at least one parent with it at the nest at all times.

Inshore feeder: a species of penguin that typically feeds within 20 km of the shore during incubation.

Monogamy: having a single partner.

Monomorphic: species in which males and females are more or less identical in external appearance. *Cf.* Sexual dimorphism, below.

Oesophageal milk: substance produced in the male emperor penguin's throat as an emergency food source if the female does not return with food for the chick by the time it hatches.

Offshore feeder: penguin that typically feeds more than 20 km from the colony during incubation, and in most instances more than 100 km away.

Post-guard stage: the period during which both parents may be away from the nest simultaneously to get food, leaving the chick unattended.

Sexual dimorphism: where males and females of a species look different, e.g. peacocks and peahens.

Subspecies: a recognised variant of a species that may have distinct characteristics and often be associated with a particular part of the range of a species, but which would freely interbreed with other members of the species.

RESOURCES

Adélie penguins are one of the most gregarious of penguins: born followers rather than leaders.

Online
New Zealand Penguins (http://www.penguin.net.nz/)
A website devoted to information about penguins of the New Zealand region.

Penguin World (http://www.penguinworld.com/)
A website with comprehensive information on all penguin species.

Publications
Campbell, H. and Hutching, G. (2007) *In Search of Ancient New Zealand*.
  Auckland: Penguin

Davis, L.S. (1993) *Penguin: a season in the life of the Adélie penguin*. London:
  Pavilion

Davis, L.S. (2001) *The Plight of the Penguin*. Dunedin: Longacre Press

Davis, L.S. (2007) *Smithsonian Q & A Penguins: the ultimate question & answer
  book*. New York: HarperCollins

Davis, L.S. and Darby, J.T. [eds] (1990) *Penguin Biology*. New York: Academic
  Press

Davis, L.S. and Renner, M. (2004) *Penguins*. New Haven: Yale University Press

Williams, T.D. (1995) *The Penguins*. Oxford: Oxford University Press

Where to see penguins in captivity in New Zealand
Auckland Zoo (www.aucklandzoo.co.nz)

Kelly Tarlton's Antarctic Encounter (www.kellytarltons.co.nz)

International Antarctic Centre, Christchurch (www.iceberg.co.nz)

INDEX

Penguins have to somehow live their lives in two worlds, with one eye to the ocean and the other to the land.

ACKNOWLEDGEMENTS

Lloyd: A big thank you to the students and colleagues who have worked with me on aspects of the biology of New Zealand's penguins: Dee Boersma, Corey Bradshaw, Christine Butts, Gordon Court, Daniel Davis, Ursula Ellenberg, Robert Harcourt, Sue Heath, Yolanda van Heezik, Dave Houston, Fiona Hunter, Robin Johnstone, Fusae Kudo, Dave Lickley, Melanie Massaro, Frances McCaffrey, Ian McLean, Shirley McQueen, Thomas Mattern, Gary Miller, Jan Murie, Kelly Nordin, Mihoko Numata, Catherine Pettigrew, Murray Potter, Martin Renner, Philip Seddon, Alvin Setiawan, Elizabeth Speirs, Nicola Vallance and Marj Wright.

Rod: The Russ family at Heritage Expeditions for generous help from Antarctica to the Equator – particularly to Rodney and Aaron for their friendship, and to those others who travelled with us and become great friends. For earlier forays into the Southern Ocean, thanks to Alex Black and family, Gerry Clark, Brian Bell and Roly Taylor. To Dr Ewan Fordyce, Department of Geology, University of Otago for his help both in the office and the field, and on Otago Peninsula John Darby, Chris Lalas, Robert Brown, Howard McGrouther, and Rod, David and Sarah McKay.